PULLING
TOGETHER

**10 RULES
FOR HIGH-
PERFORMANCE
TEAMWORK**

John J. Murphy

This publication is designed to provide accurate and authoritative information in regard to the subject matter covered. It is sold with the understanding that the publisher is not engaged in rendering legal, accounting, or other professional service. If legal advice or other expert assistance is required, the services of a competent professional person should be sought.—*From a Declaration of Principles Jointly Adopted by a Committee of the American Bar Association and a Committee of Publishers and Associations*

Photo Credits
Cover and Internals: totallyPic.com/Shutterstock

Published by Simple Truths, an imprint of Sourcebooks, Inc.
P.O. Box 4410, Naperville, Illinois 60567–4410
(630) 961-3900
Fax: (630) 961-2168
www.sourcebooks.com

Printed and bound in the United States of America.
WOZ 10 9 8 7 6 5 4 3 2 1

Teamwork is the ability to work together toward a common vision. The ability to direct individual accomplishments toward organizational objectives. It is the fuel that allows common people to attain uncommon results.

Andrew Carnegie

Contents

Introduction: Teamwork. 1

Rule #1. Put the Team First 5

Rule #2. Communicate Openly and Candidly 13

Rule #3. Be Part of the Solution, Not the Problem . . 19

Rule #4. Respect Diversity. 25

Rule #5. Ask and Encourage the Right Questions . . . 33

Rule #6. Use a Rational Problem-Solving Process . . . 41

Rule #7. Build Trust with Integrity and Example . . . 49

Rule #8. Commit to Excellence 55

Rule #9. Promote Interdependent Thinking. 63

Rule #10. Pull the Weeds 69

Lessons from the Geese 75

Behold the Power of Teamwork 79

About the Author 81

INTRODUCTION
Teamwork

Teamwork is a "principle-based" value. In other words, if you value teamwork, you have to commit to the principles that grow it. You have to sow the right seeds. You have to accept and apply the "rules of the game." True high-performance teamwork requires an extraordinary amount of trust, faith, and belief among team members, a collective mind-set that puts the team first. To cultivate this trust, a team must have something "constant" to hold on to, especially during times of change and turbulence. These "constants" give the team a foundation, a set of rules to play by. Break these rules, and you break the foundation of the team.

The purpose of this book is to clarify and explain ten rules of high-performance teamwork. These rules serve to cultivate the true power of teamwork, allowing you and your team to achieve synergistic results that exceed

anything one individual can do alone. Use this book—
and these rules—to:

- Clarify expectations and foster accountability.
- Build more focus, unity, trust, and credibility with your team.
- Align people and systems, reducing friction and accelerating flow.
- Mobilize commitment and generate enthusiasm.
- Create more balance and harmony within the team.
- Pull together and experience the extraordinary power of teamwork.

There is no limit to what can be accomplished if it doesn't matter who gets the credit.

If you value teamwork,
you have to commit to the
principles that grow it.

Put the Team First

Cooperation is the thorough conviction that nobody
can get there unless everybody gets there.

Virginia Burden

At the center of every high-performance team is a common purpose—a mission that rises above and beyond each of the individual team members. To be successful, the team's interests and needs come first. This requires *"we-opic"* vision (What's in it for we?), a challenging step-up from the common *"me-opic"* mind-set.

Effective team players understand that personal issues and personality differences are secondary to team demands. This does not mean abandoning who you are or giving up your individuality. On the contrary, it means sharing your unique strengths and differences to move the team forward. It is this we-opic focus and vision—this cooperation of collective capability—that empowers a team and generates synergy, the power of teamwork.

Cooperation means working together for mutual gain— it means sharing responsibility for success and failure and covering for one another on a moment's notice. It does not mean competing with one another at the team's expense, withholding important data or information to one-up your peers, or submitting to groupthink by going along so as not to make waves. These are rule breakers that are direct contradictions to the team-first mind-set.

High-performance teams recognize that it takes a joint effort to synergize, generating power above and beyond the collected individuals. It is with this spirit of cooperation that effective teams learn to capitalize on individual strengths and offset individual weaknesses, using diversity as an advantage.

Effective teams also understand the importance of establishing cooperative systems, structures, metrics, incentives, and rewards. We get what we inspect, not what we expect. Think about it. Do you have team job descriptions, team performance reviews, and team reward systems? Do you recognize people by pitting them against standards of excellence, or one another? What are you doing to cultivate a team-first, cooperative environment in this competitive me-opic world?

None of us is as smart as all of us.

Japanese proverb

To embrace the team-first rule, make sure your team purpose and priorities are clear.

- What is your overall mission?
- What is your game plan?
- What is expected of each team member?
- How can each member contribute most effectively?
- What constants will hold the team together?

Then stop and ask yourself, are you putting the team first?

All winning teams are goal-oriented.
Teams like these win consistently
because everyone connected with them
concentrates on specific objectives.
They go about their business with
blinders on; nothing will distract them
from achieving their aims.

Lou Holtz

A group becomes a team when each member is sure enough of himself and his contribution to praise the skills of the others.

Norman Shidle

RULE #2

Communicate Openly and Candidly

Can you imagine competing in an athletic contest without open access to the score, the clock, and the playbook? How about competing in battle without clear tactical plans and timely communication? Looking to buy a product or commission a service? How informed are the people you are considering?

Without factual information and timely, candid feedback, teams quickly dissolve into weak, dependent groups that shift responsibility and ownership for problems to those who are informed. In many organizations, this results in a crippling "dependency syndrome," an upward delegation of problem solving and conflict resolution. Got a problem? Give it to the boss to solve!

High-performance teams are empowered teams, and information is a source of great power.

With meaningful information, people can take ownership and act responsibly. Without it, people are captive. They are in the dark, doubtful about what to do and where to go.

To empower a team, begin by sharing information.

- What are the key metrics and performance indicators for the team?
- What do team members need to know on a daily, weekly, and monthly basis to manage performance responsibly?
- How do team members know the score without asking?

The word communication comes from the Latin communico, which means "to share."

While timely, candid feedback may not always be pleasant, it is necessary for any team to grow and adapt and to learn quickly from mistakes. Feedback can be verbal or visual to be effective, but never underestimate the power of self-discovery. This means designing and developing methods for team members to assess performances for themselves without micromanagement. Using self-discovery methods such as video feedback or charts that show relative performance allows team members to judge their own performances in comparison to goals, standards, trends, and/or metrics. This approach to "score keeping" creates focus, generates enthusiasm, and helps keep the team aligned. Now stop and ask yourself:

How well do you know the score?

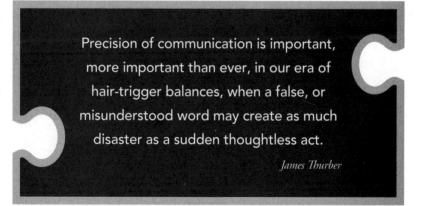

Precision of communication is important, more important than ever, in our era of hair-trigger balances, when a false, or misunderstood word may create as much disaster as a sudden thoughtless act.

James Thurber

Communicate with others as
clearly as you can to avoid
misunderstandings.

Don Miguel Ruiz

Again and again, the impossible problem is solved when we see that the problem is only a tough decision waiting to be made.

Robert H. Schuller

Be Part of the Solution, Not the Problem

Wanted: high-performance team members; passive observers need not apply. Want to be part of a winning team? Get involved. Be part of the solution, not the problem. Speak up. Share your ideas. Put the "we" in front of the "me." Volunteer your time and talents. Effective teamwork means total commitment and participation from every team member. There is no room for dead weight. Every player has an obligation to contribute, to carry part of the load. Without this commitment, a vital bond is broken. Team members have to know they can count on one another.

Effective teamwork requires that everyone leads and everyone follows from time to time, creating a powerful dynamic that invites proactive leadership. We lead when we have something important to say or contribute, using persuasion and influence to benefit the team. We follow when others are leading or when we have a plan in place. Stop and ask yourself:

- What part of the load do you carry?
- What special gifts, talents, and competencies do you offer?
- To what extent do you lead and follow effectively?
- What is your contribution?
- Remember, you do not need permission to be a team player.

There is no substitute for personal ownership, responsibility, and self-control. Accountability breeds quality performance and empowering solutions. When we take ownership for a problem and accept responsibility for our outcomes, we become agents of change as opposed to victims of change. When we resist the temptation to blame others or make excuses, we become part of the solution, not the problem.

> If we did all the things we are capable of,
> we would literally astound ourselves.
>
> *Thomas Edison*

High-performance teamwork requires self-management and self-discipline. Along with clarity in both goals and roles, effective team members understand the responsibility they each have to manage their behavior in line with team rules. This means putting the team first, sharing information, and getting involved. When everyone on the team is accountable, the team's effectiveness rises above the sum of its parts. Each team member does not just do what is asked, but what is needed.

- How are you doing in the area of personal ownership?
- Do you accept responsibility for your outcomes?
- Are you part of your team's solutions…or its problems?

Almost all employees, if they see that they will be listened to, and they have adequate information, will be able to find ways to improve their own performance and the performance of their small work group.

James O'Toole

Problems are good, not bad.
Welcome them and become
the solution.

Mark Victor Hansen

Respect Diversity

Synergy grows out of diversity. By bringing people together and encouraging a free exchange of ideas and feelings, we enrich the decision-making process. We gain insight. We get the facts. We identify options. We create alternatives. We challenge underlying assumptions and perceptions driving individual behavior. We learn about feelings, interpretations, and motives.

We provide checks and balances to one another, pooling our resources, experiences, and competencies to generate more powerful results. The secret to developing win-win solutions is to listen to the people closest to the problem, recognizing that their honest input and insight are vital to team effectiveness.

Socrates once claimed, *"You have two ears and one mouth. Use them proportionately."*

- How well do you listen? And when you are listening, to what extent are you empathizing, seeking to feel what the speaker is feeling?
- How well do you really understand and value your teammates, especially when they disagree with you?
- How well do they understand you?
- Are you listening with empathy and respecting diverse points of view? Are you communicating effectively?
- Do you have an open, honest, trusting relationship built on respect?

Effective team members recognize and appreciate the power of empathy as a vital leadership skill. They understand that influencing and motivating others, without using authority, requires respect. To inspire people, we need to tune in to what motivates them. To avoid and resolve conflict, we need to understand what annoys them. To align team members effectively, we need to assess their skills accurately. To relate well to people, we need to demonstrate that we understand and value them.

> Appreciation is a wonderful thing; it makes what
> is excellent in others belong to us as well.
>
> *Voltaire*

Healthy partnerships achieve a level of understanding beyond the norm, an almost uncanny ability to intuitively "read" each other's minds. Are you going beyond the norm? Are you connecting with your teammates? Are you listening twice as much as you speak? Assess your team and your team culture. Are team members encouraged to freely express their ideas and feelings? Do team members have a say in important decisions that impact their work? Do people feel valued and important—especially when they see things differently? Is your team using diversity to its advantage?

I have never seen a man who could do real work except under the stimulus of encouragement and enthusiasm and the approval of the people for whom he is working.

Charles Schwab

Be different—if you don't have the facts and knowledge required, simply listen. When word gets out that you can listen when others tend to talk, you will be treated as a sage.

Jim Rohn

Seek first to understand,
then to be understood.

Stephen Covey

If you take a close look at the most successful people in life, you'll find that their strength is not in having the right answers, but in asking the right questions.

John Chancellor

Ask and Encourage the Right Questions

Profound questions generate profound understanding. Questions that dig deep, really deep, open our minds to continuous learning, provocative discovery, and unlimited growth. By asking the right questions, we identify latent needs and clarify expectations. We test ourselves. We disrupt the status quo. We gain candid and valuable feedback on performance, a critical step in the cycle for ongoing improvement. We learn what we don't know. We gain insight about the market and our competition. We uncover root causes that drive results, both good and bad. We identify the critical "leverage points" governing organizational behavior. We discover opportunities for improvement. We tap into resources. We unleash the spirit of innovation and build healthier, more productive relationships.

The art of questioning is indeed a key leadership skill. It is a "pulling" technique, challenging people to think, to probe, to investigate, to challenge assumptions, and to find answers for themselves.

If you desire a wise answer, you must ask a reasonable question.

Johann Wolfgang von Goethe

Socrates used the technique so masterfully that it later became known as the Socratic method, a profound stepping-stone to enablement, empowerment, and ultimately enlightenment. Einstein, Deming, and many other thoughtful leaders used the questioning technique as well. Deliberate, profound questioning leads to innovative, profound discovery.

Building a high-performance team requires a healthy level of questioning with positive and productive intent. For example, what is the team's mission and why? What is the team's vision and why? What are the team's critical performance indicators and why? What information needs to be collected and shared?

> The important thing is not to stop questioning.
> Curiosity has its own reason for existing.
>
> *Albert Einstein*

Why? Who is on board and who is not on board? Why? What are the facts? Why are they important? What are the forces against the team? Why do they exist? What is our plan to overcome these forces? Do we have countermeasures in place? What other options do we have? What are the advantages and disadvantages of each option? What assumptions are we making? Why? What is our timeline? What resources do we need? What are our constraints? How is the team doing? What changes or adjustments do we need to make? When? Who will champion these changes? What do our customers really think of us? How do we know? What do our employees really think of us?

Do we have our priorities straight?

What really matters?

Are we asking the right questions?

To raise new questions, new possibilities, to regard old problems from a new angle requires creative imagination…

Albert Einstein

Hard work and best efforts
without guidance of profound
knowledge may well be the
root of our ruination.

W. Edwards Deming

I have found that the greatest help
in meeting any problem is to know
where you yourself stand. That is, to
have in words what you believe and
are acting from.

William Faulkner

Use a Rational Problem-Solving Process

Your team's mission is clear. So is the deadline. You begin meeting to formulate a plan. Before long, the team is at an impasse. Reaching consensus seems way out of reach. Win-win? Not today. You decide to take a vote, splitting the team into winners and losers. The majority rules. Synergy is lost. Efficiency outmaneuvers effectiveness. Feelings are hurt. Your perception of teamwork turns sour. You wonder what went wrong.

High-performance teams use a rational process when making decisions and solving problems. *The first step is to gather data, review the facts, and clearly define the problem. This critical step helps align the team upfront by getting people grounded in reality.* This is not the time for brainstorming, analyzing, and drawing conclusions. The team needs to stay on the same page and cultivate a "collective mind." *Next, the team gathers ideas, explores options, and identifies alternatives.* These first two steps are collecting steps, bonding the team together by withholding judgment and suspending disbelief.

COLLECTING STEP ONE:
GATHER DATA
REVIEW FACTS
DEFINE PROBLEM

COLLECTING STEP TWO:
GATHER IDEAS
EXPLORE OPTIONS
IDENTIFY ALTERNATIVES

Only when the team has clearly defined the situation, clarified its objectives and targets, and created multiple preliminary solutions does it move on to analysis and judgment. *When judging, effective teams use logic and human impact analysis to make a decision, carefully weighing the pros and cons of each option.* This leads to several more questions worth investigating. What could go wrong with each option? How serious would this be? How likely? Do we have countermeasures in place? What is the cost-benefit ratio for each solution? How will each solution impact the organization's culture? How will the culture impact the proposed solution? What are the forces against each option? Budgets? Timing? Resources? Constraints? How will we overcome these forces? How will we know if our proposed solution is working?

- What will we measure?
- When will we measure it?
- How will we measure it?
- And who will measure it?

**ANALYSIS/JUDGMENT
STEPS:**
ASK QUESTIONS
WEIGH PROS AND CONS

There are many different problem-solving models, all following the same basic rational sequence. This sequence is not random or without purpose. It serves to focus, align, and unite the team. The problem many teams have is that some team members are on step three while others are on step one or step four. This misalignment confuses team members, disrupts synergy, and delays results.

Are you using a rational process when you make decisions?

The significant problems
we face cannot be
solved at the same level
of thinking we were at
when we created them.

Albert Einstein

Each problem that I solved became
a rule which served afterwards to
solve other problems.

René Descartes

You must be careful how you walk,
and where you go, for there are those
following you who will set their feet
where yours are set.

Robert E. Lee

Build Trust with Integrity and Example

The greatest competitive advantages in life are those that are most difficult to copy. Anyone can put together a group of people and call them a team. Moving equipment or furniture around to colocate people is easy. Buying more equipment and furniture is even easier. Writing a mission statement? No big deal. Sharing information? In this day and age, we may be sharing too much! And if not, it's an easy fix—certainly not a sustainable competitive advantage. Designing and implementing a balanced scorecard or dashboard? It's common practice these days. Providing training? Who isn't? Negotiating benefits? Might get you agreement, which comes from the head, but it won't inspire true commitment and trust, which comes from the heart.

So, how do we get people to trust one another? Or cover for one another on a moment's notice? How do we get them to be honest with one another? Or learn from one another? How do we get team members to treat one another like winners—with value, dignity, and respect? How do we get them to put the team first? These are not quick fixes or problems we can solve with a checkbook. These are challenges that take time, dedication, and total commitment and demonstration from the leadership. These are challenges of context, not just content.

Trust is a learned behavior, as is distrust, and it is a direct reflection of the team's leadership. If you do not have trust growing in your organization, start by looking in the mirror. Are you modeling trust and integrity? Are you trustworthy? What specific evidence do you have on a day-to-day basis that proves this? How do you know? Do you demonstrate courage, fearlessness, trust, and inspiration? Is it who you are and not just what you do? Are you covering for your team members when need be? Are you openly sharing pertinent information? Are you honest and candid with your team? Do you show up on time? Do you finish on time? Do you walk your talk? Do you hold yourself personally accountable for exceeding expectations? Are you visible and approachable? Do you invite pushback and divergent points of view? Do you treat people with dignity and respect, demonstrating that you value the "me" in each individual enough to transcend the team to a "we" orientation?

- Are you learning as much from your team members as they are from you?
- What evidence do you have to support this?
- Be specific. Have examples.
- Are you putting the team first?
- Are you a positive role model? How do you know?
- Does everyone agree?

How will your team remember you?

Leadership is stirring people so they are moved from inside themselves. It is stating goals that excite them and lift their sights. It is setting the personal example, putting enthusiasm into the operation, communicating both ways (listening as well as talking).

Frederick R. Kappel

Trust is not a matter of technique, but of character. We are trusted because of our way of being, not because of our polished exteriors or our expertly crafted communications.

Marsha Sinetar

Desire is the key to motivation, but it's determination and commitment to an unrelenting pursuit of your goal —a commitment to excellence— that will enable you to attain the success you seek.

Mario Andretti

Commit to Excellence

One of the most vital bonds holding high-performance teams together is a *common commitment to excellence—a united quest for ongoing improvement.* Every player recognizes the need for raising the standards and setting new records. The marketplace does not relax. The competition is not going to let up. Customer expectations will not diminish. The glory days of the past will not protect us in the future. Each day brings with it a new challenge, an opportunity to excel beyond yesterday.

Remember that it is this perception that creates a vital link between team members, especially during times of adversity and loss. Each player must recognize a genuine commitment from one another, making mistakes more tolerable and burdens easier to carry. Committing to excellence means sharing the risk required in generating maximum returns and pursuing victory together.

PULLING TOGETHER

Effective team players know that achieving peak performance requires positive attitudes and inspiring beliefs on everyone's part. Sustaining peak performance requires humility, dignity, and grace.

Think things through and fully commit.
A halfhearted spirit has no power.
Tentative efforts lead to
tentative outcomes.

Epictetus

We are what we repeatedly do.
Excellence, then, is not an act,
but a habit.

Aristotle

Watch a competitive athlete make an honest error in a game and observe how quickly his teammates offer encouragement and support. What's this? Comfort for a mistake? A pat on the back for a mishap? How can this be? People are paid to do things right, not screw them up! Now examine your own organization. How are errors in your work environment perceived? How are mistakes handled? Are people given support for taking calculated risks and falling short? Or punished? What is the price for learning and stretching in your world?

High-performance teams view honest mistakes as part of the learning process. Given everyone on the team is committed to excellence, they review what went wrong, why it went wrong, and then focus on what needs to change. They move forward, recognizing that making no mistakes often implies they are not taking enough risks, not stretching far enough, not learning fast enough. Playing it safe does not elevate people to peak performance. We have to dare to get a hit, recognizing that "striking out" is part of the same process. Give it some thought.

- Are you stepping up to the plate?
- Are you putting your heart and soul into your work?
- Do your teammates honestly believe you are giving everything you can?

When you look in the mirror, do you see a person committed to excellence, a tenacious team member striving for total quality?

Great discoveries and
achievements invariably
involve the cooperation
of many minds.

Alexander Graham Bell

Thinkers help others to think, for they formulate what others are thinking. No person writes or thinks alone—thought is in the air but its expression is necessary to create a tangible spirit of the times.

Elbert Hubbard

Promote Interdependent Thinking

High-performance teamwork is not a dependent process where people abandon the "me" and cling to the team for identity and support. Nor is it an independent process where the "me" comes first. High-performance teamwork is an interdependent process where team members rise to a level of sharing, accepting, giving, and going beyond oneself. This means showing up on time, paying attention, asking for and providing help, offering encouragement and support, valuing diversity, and viewing one another as important to the team.

Each day we are challenged to do whatever we do better, faster, cheaper, and with more ease. And, in many cases, we are challenged to innovate and transform, to completely shift paradigms and replace the old way with something entirely new. It is through high-performance teamwork, and mindful, interdependent thinking, that we raise the bar and set new standards. It is also through synergistic decision-making that we close the gaps that exist in organizations with stagnant, isolated, defensive, independent thinking.

The emphasis today is on seamlessly providing value to customers through value streams. For many organizations, this means reengineering slow, vertical, hierarchies into fast, horizontal, multiskilled units, giving team ownership and accountability for processes from start to finish. For team members, this often means cross-training to learn multiple skills, not just a single, functional skill. Consider the game of basketball, a very fast, dynamic environment. Notice that all of the players can perform all of the skills, allowing them to cover for one another quickly and spontaneously. Anything less would be costly. Indeed, each player has a position with an assignment, but it is not so rigid that we observe players "pointing fingers" or claiming "it's not my job." Thinking interdependently means shifting from "what's in it for me?" to "what's in it for we?"

> The biggest lesson I have ever learned is the stupendous importance of what we think. If I knew what you think, I would know what you are, for your thoughts make you what you are. By changing our thoughts, we can change our lives.
>
> *Dale Carnegie*

Want to be empowered in this day and age? Think interdependently. Begin by enabling and empowering yourself. Think outside your own self-limiting box to expand your knowledge. Talk with and listen to experts. Find yourself a positive role model. Benchmark against the best. Ask a lot of questions. Seek to understand. Get on the Internet. Read a book. Listen to an audio program. Solicit the help of a peer or mentor. Look at the big picture. The only barrier to lifelong learning and interdependent thinking is you. Reorganize your time to recognize education and learning as a priority. Volunteer to learn new jobs and skills. Get past your own ego and self-imposed restrictions. The resources are all around you.

Ask yourself, are you willing to step up? Are you looking beyond your existing position and limiting excuses? Do you see how your job fits into something larger? Do you see how interdependent you are?

Build for your team a feeling of oneness, of dependence on one another and of strength to be derived by unity.

Vincent Lombardi

Team members have to be focused on the collective good of the team. Too often, they focus their attention on their department, their budget, their career aspirations, their egos.

Patrick Lencioni

Pull the Weeds

Like the gardener, the effective team leader recognizes that cultivating teamwork takes time and commitment. Pulling up the "roots" before the process has matured is a sure way to confuse people and destroy what has been started. To grow a healthy team, learn to trust the rules and allow the process to take its course.

The vital components to teamwork take time to develop and grow—trust, open communication, "we-opic" vision, healthy self-esteem, dignity, interdependent growth, participation, sharing, cooperation. Even the most effective team members have conflicts arising from tempers, greed, selfishness, ego, fear, and insecurity. This is why patience and perseverance are also vitally important. The healthy team recognizes that people are people. We have off days. We make mistakes. We have doubts. We assume too much. We differ. This is where great teams distinguish themselves from all the rest. They see these differences as advantages, not excuses to give up. They understand that patience and perseverance are great virtues, the mark of extraordinary wisdom and strength. Plant the right seeds, respect the growing process, and behold the power of teamwork. Great teams also understand that life is full of choices. Some people choose to accept and "play by the rules," and others do not.

Keep in mind, teamwork is a value. Some people value it, honoring the truths that create it. Others reject it, insisting that these rules are not important. Effective team leaders understand that they have an obligation to align each team member responsibly. Anything less destroys the trust, credibility, and respect required to build an effective team. Obstacles and "weeds" must be removed in order for efficient growth to take place. A weed is someone who refuses to accept these rules, choosing instead to behave independently of the team. Weeds make their own rules, undermining team consensus. A weed expects double standards. A weed refuses to share and participate. A weed shifts responsibility to others and rejects accountability. A weed looks upon these rules as a disruption, as an annoyance to getting a job done.

Do not be fooled. Weeds may seem harmless. They may even blossom from time to time. But a weed cannot be trusted. Beneath the surface, it is doing everything it can to take over your garden.

Pull the weeds and give everyone else some room to grow. Think about it—does your team need a little cultivating?

I am a member of a team, and I rely on the team, I defer to it and sacrifice for it, because the team, not the individual, is the ultimate champion.

Mia Hamm

We must cultivate our garden.

Candide

Lessons from the Geese

Consistent application of the ten rules of high-performance teamwork ultimately generates trust, respect, unity, and power within any team. Conversely, consistent violation of any one rule destroys this bond. "Lessons From the Geese" by Dr. Robert McNeish is a powerful illustration from nature of the rules of high-performance teamwork. As you read about the natural unity that exists among this species remember—this same unity can exist in your organization!

As geese flap their wings, they create an uplift for the bird following. By flying in a V formation, the whole flock adds 71 percent greater flying range than if any bird were to fly alone.

If we share a common direction and a sense of community, we can get where we are going more quickly and easily because we are traveling on the thrust of one another!

Whenever a goose falls out of formation, it suddenly feels the drag and resistance of trying to fly alone, and quickly gets back into formation to take advantage of the lifting power of the bird immediately in front.

If we have as much sense as geese, we will stay in formation with those who are headed where we want to go, and we will be willing to accept their help as well as give help to others.

When the lead goose gets tired, it rotates back into formation and another goose flies at the point position.

If we take turns doing the hard tasks and sharing leadership, as with the geese, we become interdependent with one another.

The geese in formation honk from behind to encourage those up front to keep up their speed.

If we "honk," we need to make sure it is positive and encouraging. When a goose gets sick or wounded or is shot down, two geese drop out of formation and follow it down to help and protect it. They stay with it until it is able to fly again or dies. They then launch out on their own, with another formation or catch up with the flock.

If we have as much sense as geese, we too will stand by each other in difficult times, as well as when we are strong. Let us all try to fly in formation and remember to drop back to help those who might need it!

Behold the Power
of Teamwork

The greatest accomplishments in life are not achieved by individuals alone, but by proactive people pulling together for a common good. Look behind every winner and you will find a great coach. Look out in front of every superstar and you will see a positive role model. Look alongside every great achiever and you will find caring people offering encouragement, support, and able assistance.

Rising to this level of interdependent thinking can be challenging and difficult. Looking beyond oneself, asking for help or accepting help can feel risky. But people are not given life to simply take from one another. We are here to give. *Our mission in life is to offer our gifts to benefit one another, to create mutual gain in the world.* This is called teamwork—a win-win mind-set stemming from a genuine commitment to the rules that allow it to happen.

About the Author

John J. Murphy is a highly recognized author, speaker, and management consultant. Drawing on a diverse collection of team experiences as a corporate manager, consultant, and collegiate quarterback, John has appeared on over four hundred radio and television stations and his work has been featured in over fifty newspapers nationwide.

As founder and president of Venture Management Consultants (www.venturemangementconsultants.com), John specializes in creating high-performance team environments, teaching leadership and team development, and leading team Kaizen events. He has trained thousands of "change agents" from over fifty countries and helped some of the world's leading organizations design and implement positive change.

John is a critically acclaimed author and sought-after

speaker. Among his other books are: *Beyond Doubt: Four Steps to Inner Peace*; *Reinvent Yourself: A Lesson in Personal Leadership*; *Agent of Change: Leading a Cultural Revolution*; *Get a Real Life: A Lesson in Personal Empowerment*; *The Eight Disciplines: An Enticing Look into Your Personality*; *Zentrepreneur: Get Out of the Way and Lead, Create a Culture of Innovation and Fearlessness*; and *Leapfrogging the Competition* with Mac Anderson.

Book Discussion Questions

1. In what ways do we demonstrate a "we-opic" vision at our company or in our department? Why is this important?

   _____

   _____

   _____

   _____

   _____

2. Give an example of "groupthink" and explain why this is counterproductive to establishing a high-performance team?

   _____

   _____

   _____

   _____

   _____

3. How is "dependency syndrome" created, and how can we avoid it? Why is this important?

_____

_____

_____

_____

_____

4. What are some examples of how we can give direction to another team member in a way that is empowering rather than micromanaging? Why is this important in assessing performance?

_____

_____

_____

_____

_____

5. A rich exchange of ideas depends on diversity and open communication. Why is this essential for a team? Give a specific example of a solution or action that was the direct result of team diversity.

    _____

    _____

    _____

    _____

    _____

6. When faced with solving a problem, which is more likely to produce the strongest result: thinking like a collective mind or thinking with independent minds. Why? How is this different from groupthink?

    _____

    _____

    _____

    _____

    _____

7. It is important to demonstrate a commitment to excellence. Describe the ways that show we are committed to excellence. Where do we come up short and what can we do about it now?

_____

_____

_____

_____

_____

8. How should we approach mistakes? Is there value to be gained from a mistake? Give an example.

_____

_____

_____

_____

_____

9. What is the difference between independent thinking and interdependent thinking? How can we as individuals empower ourselves and learn to think interdependently? Give examples.

   _____

   _____

   _____

   _____

   _____

10. How is building high-performance teamwork like cultivating a garden? What are the seeds that sow a healthy team? If we value high-performance teamwork and results, what must we commit to up front?

    _____

    _____

    _____

    _____

    _____

11. What is a weed, and how is a weed a barrier to healthy growth as a team?

   _____

   _____

   _____

   _____

   _____

   _____